# An Entrepreneur's Guide to Advertising

A 52 week Guide to Advertising for the Aspiring and Established Entrepreneur

Kevin T. Karr

# Copyright

Copyright Kevin T. Karr © 2016. No part of this publication may be replicated, redistributed, or given away in any form without the prior written consent of the author / publisher or the terms relayed to you herin.

This journal is intended for use by entrepreneurs who wish to keep a journal of their advertising ideas. Various ideas and locations may be documented within the pages of this journal, and it is meant to serve as a guide and reference book to established and aspiring entrepreneurs alike.

# Products and Target Markets

This page is a list of the various products to be advertised, as well as the target market for those products.

_____
_____
_____
_____
_____
_____
_____
_____
_____
_____
_____
_____
_____
_____
_____
_____
_____

# Location Ideas to Reach Specified Target Market

- Billboards
- Television
- Radio
- Web pages
- Social media
- Mailers
- _____
- _____
- _____
- _____
- _____
- _____
- _____

# Location Idea

Location _____
Date_____
Product _____
Target Market_____

Advertisement Idea:

_____
_____
_____
_____
_____
_____
_____
_____
_____
_____

# Location Idea

Location _____

Date _____

Product _____

Target Market _____

Advertisement Idea:

_____
_____
_____
_____
_____
_____
_____
_____
_____
_____

# Location Idea

Location _____
Date _____
Product _____
Target Market _____

Advertisement Idea:
_____
_____
_____
_____
_____
_____
_____
_____
_____
_____
_____
_____

# Location Idea

Location _____

Date_____

Product _____

Target Market_____

Advertisement Idea:

_____
_____
_____
_____
_____
_____
_____
_____
_____
_____

# Location Idea

Location _____

Date _____

Product _____

Target Market _____

Advertisement Idea:

_____
_____
_____
_____
_____
_____
_____
_____
_____
_____
_____

# Location Idea

Location _____

Date _____

Product _____

Target Market _____

Advertisement Idea:

_____
_____
_____
_____
_____
_____
_____
_____
_____
_____
_____

# Location Idea

Location _____

Date_____

Product _____

Target Market_____

Advertisement Idea:

_____
_____
_____
_____
_____
_____
_____
_____
_____
_____
_____
_____

# Location Idea

Location _____

Date _____

Product _____

Target Market _____

Advertisement Idea:

_____
_____
_____
_____
_____
_____
_____
_____
_____
_____

# Location Idea

Location _____

Date _____

Product _____

Target Market _____

Advertisement Idea:

_____
_____
_____
_____
_____
_____
_____
_____
_____
_____

# Location Idea

Location _____

Date _____

Product _____

Target Market _____

Advertisement Idea:

_____
_____
_____
_____
_____
_____
_____
_____
_____
_____

# Location Idea

Location _____

Date _____

Product _____

Target Market _____

Advertisement Idea:

_____
_____
_____
_____
_____
_____
_____
_____
_____
_____
_____
_____

# Location Idea

Location _____

Date _____

Product _____

Target Market _____

Advertisement Idea:

_____
_____
_____
_____
_____
_____
_____
_____
_____
_____
_____

# Location Idea

Location _____

Date_____

Product _____

Target Market_____

Advertisement Idea:

_____
_____
_____
_____
_____
_____
_____
_____
_____
_____
_____

# Location Idea

Location _____

Date_____

Product _____

Target Market_____

Advertisement Idea:

_____
_____
_____
_____
_____
_____
_____
_____
_____
_____
_____

# Location Idea

Location _____

Date _____

Product _____

Target Market _____

Advertisement Idea:

_____
_____
_____
_____
_____
_____
_____
_____
_____
_____
_____

# Location Idea

Location _____

Date _____

Product _____

Target Market _____

Advertisement Idea:

_____
_____
_____
_____
_____
_____
_____
_____
_____
_____

# Location Idea

Location _____

Date _____

Product _____

Target Market _____

Advertisement Idea:

_____
_____
_____
_____
_____
_____
_____
_____
_____
_____
_____

# Location Idea

Location _____

Date _____

Product _____

Target Market _____

Advertisement Idea:

_____
_____
_____
_____
_____
_____
_____
_____
_____
_____
_____

# Location Idea

Location _____
Date_____
Product _____
Target Market_____

Advertisement Idea:

_____
_____
_____
_____
_____
_____
_____
_____
_____
_____
_____

# Location Idea

Location _____

Date _____

Product _____

Target Market _____

Advertisement Idea:

_____
_____
_____
_____
_____
_____
_____
_____
_____
_____
_____

# Location Idea

Location _____

Date _____

Product _____

Target Market _____

Advertisement Idea:

_____

_____

_____

_____

_____

_____

_____

_____

_____

_____

# Location Idea

Location _____

Date _____

Product _____

Target Market _____

Advertisement Idea:

_____
_____
_____
_____
_____
_____
_____
_____
_____
_____

# Location Idea

Location _____

Date _____

Product _____

Target Market _____

Advertisement Idea:

_____

_____

_____

_____

_____

_____

_____

_____

_____

_____

_____

# Location Idea

Location _____

Date_____

Product _____

Target Market_____

Advertisement Idea:

_____
_____
_____
_____
_____
_____
_____
_____
_____
_____
_____

# Location Idea

Location _____

Date _____

Product _____

Target Market _____

Advertisement Idea:

_____
_____
_____
_____
_____
_____
_____
_____
_____
_____

# Location Idea

Location _____

Date _____

Product _____

Target Market _____

Advertisement Idea:

_____
_____
_____
_____
_____
_____
_____
_____
_____
_____
_____
_____

# Location Idea

Location _____

Date _____

Product _____

Target Market _____

Advertisement Idea:

_____

_____

_____

_____

_____

_____

_____

_____

_____

_____

_____

# Location Idea

Location _____

Date_____

Product _____

Target Market_____

Advertisement Idea:

_____
_____
_____
_____
_____
_____
_____
_____
_____
_____
_____

# Location Idea

Location _____

Date _____

Product _____

Target Market _____

Advertisement Idea:

_____
_____
_____
_____
_____
_____
_____
_____
_____
_____
_____

# Location Idea

Location _____

Date_____

Product _____

Target Market_____

Advertisement Idea:

_____

_____

_____

_____

_____

_____

_____

_____

_____

_____

# Location Idea

Location _____

Date _____

Product _____

Target Market _____

Advertisement Idea:

_____
_____
_____
_____
_____
_____
_____
_____
_____
_____
_____
_____

# Location Idea

Location _____

Date _____

Product _____

Target Market _____

Advertisement Idea:

_____
_____
_____
_____
_____
_____
_____
_____
_____
_____
_____
_____
_____

# Location Idea

Location _____
Date_____
Product _____
Target Market_____

Advertisement Idea:
_____
_____
_____
_____
_____
_____
_____
_____
_____
_____
_____
_____

# Location Idea

Location _____

Date _____

Product _____

Target Market _____

Advertisement Idea:

_____
_____
_____
_____
_____
_____
_____
_____
_____
_____

# Location Idea

Location _____

Date _____

Product _____

Target Market _____

Advertisement Idea:

_____

_____

_____

_____

_____

_____

_____

_____

_____

_____

# Location Idea

Location _____

Date _____

Product _____

Target Market _____

Advertisement Idea:

_____
_____
_____
_____
_____
_____
_____
_____
_____
_____
_____

# Location Idea

Location _____
Date_____
Product _____
Target Market_____

Advertisement Idea:

_____
_____
_____
_____
_____
_____
_____
_____
_____
_____
_____

# Location Idea

Location _____

Date _____

Product _____

Target Market _____

Advertisement Idea:

_____

_____

_____

_____

_____

_____

_____

_____

_____

_____

_____

# Location Idea

Location _____

Date_____

Product _____

Target Market_____

Advertisement Idea:

_____

_____

_____

_____

_____

_____

_____

_____

_____

_____

_____

# Location Idea

Location _____

Date _____

Product _____

Target Market _____

Advertisement Idea:

_____
_____
_____
_____
_____
_____
_____
_____
_____
_____

# Location Idea

Location _____

Date _____

Product _____

Target Market _____

Advertisement Idea:

_____

_____

_____

_____

_____

_____

_____

_____

_____

_____

_____

# Location Idea

Location _____

Date_____

Product _____

Target Market_____

Advertisement Idea:

_____
_____
_____
_____
_____
_____
_____
_____
_____
_____

# Location Idea

Location _____

Date _____

Product _____

Target Market _____

Advertisement Idea:

_____

_____

_____

_____

_____

_____

_____

_____

_____

_____

# Location Idea

Location _____

Date_____

Product _____

Target Market_____

Advertisement Idea:

_____
_____
_____
_____
_____
_____
_____
_____
_____
_____
_____

# Location Idea

Location _____

Date_____

Product _____

Target Market_____

Advertisement Idea:

_____
_____
_____
_____
_____
_____
_____
_____
_____
_____

# Location Idea

Location _____

Date _____

Product _____

Target Market _____

Advertisement Idea:

_____
_____
_____
_____
_____
_____
_____
_____
_____
_____
_____

# Location Idea

Location _____

Date_____

Product _____

Target Market_____

Advertisement Idea:

_____

_____

_____

_____

_____

_____

_____

_____

_____

# Location Idea

Location _____

Date_____

Product _____

Target Market_____

Advertisement Idea:

_____

_____

_____

_____

_____

_____

_____

_____

_____

# Location Idea

Location _____

Date_____

Product _____

Target Market_____

Advertisement Idea:

_____
_____
_____
_____
_____
_____
_____
_____
_____
_____
_____
_____

# Location Idea

Location _____

Date_____

Product _____

Target Market_____

Advertisement Idea:

_____
_____
_____
_____
_____
_____
_____
_____
_____
_____

# Location Idea

Location _____

Date _____

Product _____

Target Market _____

Advertisement Idea:

_____
_____
_____
_____
_____
_____
_____
_____
_____
_____
_____

# Location Idea

Location _____

Date _____

Product _____

Target Market _____

Advertisement Idea:

_____
_____
_____
_____
_____
_____
_____
_____
_____
_____

# Location Idea

Location _____

Date _____

Product _____

Target Market _____

Advertisement Idea:

_____
_____
_____
_____
_____
_____
_____
_____
_____
_____
_____
_____

Thank you for purchasing this journal we hope you find it invaluable in all of your entrepreneurial endeavors. Please look for our other publications coming in the future.

www.ingramcontent.com/pod-product-compliance
Lightning Source LLC
Chambersburg PA
CBHW061447180526
45170CB00004B/1599